FEMALE ATHLETES

WOMEN
IN THE
WORLD™

FEMALE
ATHLETES

LENA KOYA AND LAURA LA BELLA

Rosen
YA

TM

New York

Published in 2018 by The Rosen Publishing Group, Inc.
29 East 21st Street, New York, NY 10010

First Edition

Library of Congress Cataloging-in-Publication Data

Names: Koya, Lena, author. | La Bella, Laura, author.
Title: Female athletes / Lena Koya and Laura La Bella.
Description: New York, NY : Rosen Publishing, 2018 | Series: Women in the world | Audience: Grades 7–12. | Includes bibliographical references and index.
Identifiers: LCCN 2017011967 | ISBN 9781508177180 (library bound) | ISBN 9781508178552 (paperback)
Subjects: LCSH: Sports for women—Juvenile literature.
Classification: LCC GV709 .K65 2018 | DDC 796.082—dc23
LC record available at https://lccn.loc.gov/2017011967

Manufactured in China

CONTENTS

More and more female athletes are becoming household names. It's easy to remember the superstars, including soccer player Abby Wambach, NASCAR driver Danica Patrick, and Grand Slam tennis aces Venus and Serena Williams. And there are many more female athletes who impress viewers around the world with their skill, strength, determination, and endurance.

These women are tremendously successful. They are sought after for multi-million-dollar endorsement deals with the largest companies in the world. They star in advertisements and are featured on the pages of magazines. They win prestigious prizes and travel all over the world. But it is important to not forget that these women are also fighting for greater recognition for their hard work in a male-dominated world—the world of sports. Not too long ago, women were absent on the fields of professional sports. This doesn't mean that they weren't capable of playing or that they didn't want to play, but rather their access to professional sports was restricted. As

little as seventy years ago, women were not allowed to play in many major competitions for sports including track and field, swimming, and baseball. This began to change in the 1950s and 1960s, when professional sports organizations for women began, including the

Abby Wambach, shown here celebrating the US women's national soccer team's World Cup victory in 2015, is one of the most successful female athletes in the world.

Ladies' Professional Golf Association (LPGA). Some women fought for greater opportunities in sports competition by unofficially registering for men's events or even competing in disguise. But it was an uphill battle. In many ways, women athletes continue to fight for greater accessibility and rights in sports today.

Despite the successes of athletes like the Williams sisters, Patrick, and Wambach, among many others, female athletes continue to face challenges today. They experience greater discrimination in sports and are often judged by their physical appearance rather than their athletic abilities. They face pressures that many male athletes do not. They are often paid less for winning major competitions than their male counterparts are. And, from a young age, many young women are discouraged from professional sports and are provided with far fewer opportunities than young men.

The stress that many female athletes face because of their gender causes unique challenges. Unfortunately, many female athletes suffer from eating disorders, increased alcohol use, and increased rates of depression and anxiety. A great deal of this is fueled by the way the media treats female athletes. While male athletes are often lauded in the media for their athletic prowess, female athletes are often displayed as little more than eye candy for a largely male audience. It can be devastating for women who have dedicated their entire lives to reaching the top of their chosen sport, making them feel as if they are only appreciated for their physique.

But female athletes continue to struggle against these odds—and succeed. Every year, more women participate in sports at all levels. These women are actively fighting against the stereotype that women are weaker than men, less interested in sports, and less athletically skilled. Their sporting performances prove what women can be successful and will serve as inspiration for future generations of women who have the strength, skill, and sheer willpower to make it in the world of sports.

CHAPTER 1

A HISTORY OF WOMEN IN SPORTS

The first Olympic Games were held in ancient Greece in 776 BC to celebrate athletic prowess and strength. Only male athletes could take part in this most prestigious sporting event and women weren't even allowed to observe from the stands. In protest, women organized their own sporting competition, called the Heraean Games in honor of the goddess Hera. They competed every four years before the men's events, typically in foot races.

Fast forward to the modern Olympic Games, where every two years the world watches as some of the most powerful female athletes

Women were originally left out of the Olympic Games in ancient Greece. Here, women dressed as priestesses reenact the ancient ritual of lighting the Olympic torch.

gather to compete in events as diverse as swimming, skiing, figure skating, gymnastics, ice hockey, speed skating, soccer, cycling, weightlifting, and track and field. On display are feats of outstanding athletic skill, endurance, strength, agility, and speed. Much has changed for the women at the Olympics, and for female athletes everywhere.

FIGHTING FOR EQUALITY IN ATHLETICS

Women have been excelling at athletics for centuries. In the 1550s, Mary, Queen of Scots, was known to be an avid golfer. In 1858, Julia Archibald Holmes climbed Pike's Peak in Colorado. Women's college basketball and baseball teams date back to the 1860s. Then, many of these activities were more recreational than competitive. At the time it was believed that women should not, and could not, exert themselves physically.

But women knew better. As they continued to insist on their right to play sports, women's clubs and intermural teams cropped up at colleges all over the country. The women's suffrage movement in the late nineteenth and early twentieth centuries eventually lead to the Nineteenth Amendment, giving women the right to vote. It wasn't until this time that women felt empowered to pursue other freedoms, including their equal right to compete in athletics.

At first, women's engagement in sports was limited. Sweating, physical contact, and competition were not "ladylike" behaviors, so opportunities for women to be athletic were restricted to sports like golf, archery, and croquet. These activities were among the first sports considered acceptable for women because they were not strenuous, nor did they involve physical contact.

CATHARINE BEECHER'S EXERCISE MANUAL FOR WOMEN

In 1860, the educator and activist Catharine Beecher published the first exercise manual for women. During this time, physical exercise was deemed "unwomanly" and upper-class women were discouraged from participating in any kind of sports. In her manual—

(continued on the next page)

Catharine Beecher, seated second from left with her famous family, was an early advocate of women's physical activity.

(continued from the previous page)

the first of its kind—Beecher included different exercises for different parts of the body along with diagrams. She linked the physical health of women to their mental health and encouraged women to get healthy in order to teach their daughters the benefits of physical activity. Later, Beecher went on to advocate for the inclusion of physical education in women's schools. For Beecher, physical education was a way of empowering her fellow women.

The pursuit of women's equality in sports took a big leap forward during World War II. In the 1940s, many men entered the military to fight in the war, leaving women behind to fill their positions in factories and in the workplace. This gave women the opportunity to prove they were equal to men in the workforce and could handle working outside the home while managing their roles as homemakers. These new roles also gave women the self-esteem and confidence to push for full equal rights.

The war not only brought women into the workforce, it also led to the first women's professional baseball league. At the time, since so many young men

Two outfielders in the All-American Girls Baseball League reach to catch a ball. Women were recruited to play professional sports while men fought abroad in World War II.

were drafted for the war, Major League Baseball was canceled. Baseball league executives were looking for a way to keep the sport in the public eye while its male stars were away fighting the war. Philip K. Wrigley, owner of the Wrigley chewing-gum company and the Chicago Cubs, gathered other baseball executives and started a new professional league with women players.

In 1943, the All-American Girls Baseball League was created. The league, whose story was featured in the 1992 Hollywood film *A League of Their Own*, was popular with fans. Wrigley emphasized the importance of being feminine and projecting the image of "The All-American Girl Next Door," all while featuring players with outstanding athletic ability. The league included fifteen teams, and each season culminated with a league championship. The league stayed in operation until 1954.

After World War II ended, and still riding the popularity of the women's baseball league, organizations for women in sports began to increase. Women's athletics became more competitive, and intercollegiate and interscholastic competition spread. This movement would eventually lead to Title IX, federal legislation that would help to equalize the opportunities for and treatment of women in athletics.

TITLE IX COMPLIANCE

Title IX, officially known as the Patsy Mink Equal Opportunity in Education Act, was passed in 1972 and changed the way athletics departments around the United States were run. It states, in part, "No person in the United States shall, on the basis of sex, be excluded from participation in, be denied the benefits of, or be subjected to discrimination under any education program or activity receiving Federal financial assistance."

In order to determine if a school complies with Title IX, a three-part test is often used. First, schools must make sure that they provide opportunities for participation in sports that are proportionate to the gender composition of their student population. Second, schools must show that they are continually trying to improve athletic opportunities for the underrepresented gender (typically female) in sports. Third, and finally, they must accommodate the interests of the underrepresented gender. Thus, if there are fewer female students in a school than male students, but the majority of this group is interested in starting a particular sports team, the school is obligated to provide this opportunity.

THE FIGHT FOR EQUALITY CONTINUES

Even though Title IX helped to level the playing field between men and women in sports, the struggle for recognition and equality continues to this day. According to the Women's Sports Foundation, the number of women athletes in college has increased by more than 600 percent since the passage of Title IX. However, women's college sports teams still receive much less money than men's teams, at an average of just 39.6 percent of overall athletic expenses. And, according to data from the National Federation of State High School Associations, high schools provide girls with 1.3 million fewer opportunities to play sports than boys.

Even the structure of organized athletics today, from youth leagues to the Olympics, supports a belief that women can't play as long or as hard as men. The false assumption that women are physically inferior to men has led to a sharp gender division in sports. For example, in tennis matches, women play three games while men play five. In golf, women start closer to the hole than men do, and in youth leagues girls play nine holes while boys play the full eighteen. These notions suggest that men's sports are to be taken more seriously then women's sports and that women don't have the power, stamina, or ability to compete equally with men.

While physical differences exist between men and women, they should not dictate rules for endurance. Instead, these physical differences should only inspire a different set of rules for those sports in which extremely physical contact occurs, such as football or boxing, where the physical strength of male and female athletes is not equal and could lead to an unfair advantage or injury if co-ed play were allowed. But in sports where such physical power has little if any influence, specific gender-based rules are unnecessary.

Co-ed adult sports leagues are the perfect example of how these gender rules are senseless and unnecessary. In some co-ed basketball leagues, women earn two points for every basket while men earn only one. Co-ed softball leagues are known to enforce rules such as having no more than two men bat in a row. Sometimes men are pitched larger balls while women are pitched smaller ones. These rules assume that men are better athletes than women or that women need to be given an advantage because they don't have the ability to play by a more demanding and rigorous set of rules.

The University of Connecticut's women's basketball team would argue that a separate and less stringent set of rules is not needed for women to

The UConn Huskies have proved again and again that female athletes can compete at the same levels as male athletes.

prove their dominance in a sporting event. From 2014 through 2017, the Huskies won 111 games in a row, breaking their own previous record of 90 consecutive wins. This, in turn, broke the previous record streak of 88 games set by the 1970s-era UCLA men's team. In basketball, the court isn't smaller for women, the quarters of play aren't shorter, and the points awarded for baskets are the same.

CHAPTER 2

GENDER ROLES IN SPORTS

During an infamous incident in 2009, University of New Mexico women's soccer defender Elizabeth Lambert was suspended for the remainder of the season after video emerged of her playing roughly in a game against Brigham Young University. Throughout the game, Lambert elbowed, kicked, and punched players from the opposing team—even pulling a Brigham Young player to the ground by her ponytail. Following this incident, video showing Lambert's "misbehavior" on the field became viral. Lambert was even invited to speak on *The Today Show*. Lambert suggested that other

The 2009 scandal around Elizabeth Lambert's behavior on the soccer field highlighted how differently the media and spectators view women's and men's sports.

players had been just as physical as she had during the game and that she had elicited such a negative response because soccer fans were not used to seeing women play as roughly as men on the field.

Division I soccer is a physical contact sport, for both men's and women's teams. In men's soccer, we see forceful, sometimes hostile physical performances, but none seem to gain the media attention that Lambert's actions did. Could it be that we don't expect a pretty, young female athlete to act in a violent, aggressive manner?

What happens when female athletes are too good or play aggressively like male athletes? Society has a difficult time accepting women as formidable, assertive athletes.

WHAT ARE GENDER ROLES?

If Elizabeth Lambert had been a male player, it's likely that the footage of her actions in the soccer game would not have gone viral on the internet. It's also unlikely that a male player would have been assaulted verbally and threatened in blogs and in email messages as Lambert was. But Lambert is far from the first female athlete to exhibit confrontational actions during a sporting event. In fact, these types of actions aren't uncommon in women's sports. Lambert's situation illustrates a continuing challenge female athletes face: when being competitive, is there a place for traditional notions of femininity in sports?

In 2008, eleven Women's National Basketball Association (WNBA) players were suspended after a shoving match between the Los Angeles Sparks and the Detroit Shock. That same year, Serena Williams verbally assaulted and threatened a US Open line judge after she disagreed with a call. Both of these incidents attracted national attention. Yet, we regularly

When tennis star Serena Williams aggressively disagreed with a US Open line judge's call, she drew negative attention from spectators and fans who viewed her behavior as inappropriate.

see examples of physical confrontation in men's sports, from fistfights in hockey games and trash talking on the basketball court of an National Basketball Association (NBA) game to a bounty system that rewards violent hits that knock opposing players out of the football game in the NFL. Society rarely questions when a male player acts inappropriately, but when a female athlete does, she is labeled unladylike. Aggressive female athletes are called emotionally unbalanced, hysterical, irrational, or unnatural. When female athletes demonstrate characteristics that go against what society deems "ladylike" behavior, traditional gender roles are challenged.

Gender roles are a set of social behaviors that are considered appropriate for individuals of a specific sex. Traditional gender roles expect men to be rational, strong, hard working, and masculine. Women are expected to be domestic, nurturing, feminine, and emotional. Gender roles are often used to tell people how they are supposed to act, look, and even what one's interests should be. Little girls are given dolls and play kitchens as toys, while little boys receive trucks and sporting equipment.

Athletes in particular are often evaluated and judged by the very narrow and confining criteria of traditional gender roles. Women and girls who excel in sports challenge society's perception of the way women and girls are supposed to act and what they are supposed to be interested in. When we see an athlete like Lambert acting physically, aggressively, or even violently on a playing field, it goes against how society expects a woman to behave. Although it has become somewhat more acceptable for female athletes to participate in traditionally male-dominated sports, such as hockey, wrestling, or boxing, there is a lingering negative connotation attached to those female athletes who attempt to do so. When women exhibit what society considers more manly traits, they

GENDER IDENTITY AND SPORTS

One way in which gender roles play out in sports is through the treatment of transgender athletes by professional sports organizations. Beginning in the 1940s, sports organizations required "sex verification" to prove that athletes who competed in women's sports competitions were cisgender women—that their gender expression corresponded with the sex assigned at their birth. This could be done through hormone testing, chromosomal analysis, or even visual inspection of genitals. Unfortunately, this practice continues today and has excluded many transgender athletes from participating in professional sports.

The fight for trans equality in sports continues to this day. In 2004, the International Olympics Committee (IOC) officially allowed transgender athletes to participate in the Olympic Games. In 2015, the IOC changed guidelines that had previously required athletes to undergo gender affirmation surgery. The new guidelines for transgender athletes stipulate that female trans athletes must declare their gender four years previous to competing and that they maintain a certain level of testosterone.

face questions about their gender identity, sexual orientation, values, and social roles.

STEREOTYPES ABOUT FEMALE ATHLETES

Female athletes with skills that are typically considered "male characteristics," such as speed and strength, can have image problems. Society does not know how to view or portray these female athletes.

When the US Women's soccer team won the World Cup in 2015, they received a great deal of media attention. However, some journalists chose to focus less on their accomplishments in sports and more on their personal or family lives. For example, an article published in *The Atlantic* focused on the US women's soccer players as mothers; titled "The Soccer Moms," it showed photographs of the women with their partners and children instead of action shots

The US women's soccer team is one of the most decorated sports teams in history, although media attention on individual players has often focused on their physical attributes and family lives, instead of their athletic abilities.

from the World Cup. Research has shown that by featuring female athletes in more traditional gender roles—in this case, as wives, girlfriends, or mothers—they become more acceptable to the public. In many cases, female athletes must prove they live their lives off the field according to traditional gender roles. For female athletes who either appear more masculine or exhibit exceptional athletic ability, questions about their sexual orientation often arise. Many female athletes face questions about their sexuality or insinuations that they are gay. Media coverage of men's sports focuses on their athletic accomplishments, while female athletes's personal and domestic lives are included in profiles of their athletic successes.

Abby Wambach was the 2011 Associated Press Athlete of the Year. She is a star of the women's US World Cup soccer team and is among soccer's top five highest goal scorers. She's one of the most decorated female soccer players of all time and one of the world's most recognizable soccer players. When she began garnering international attention for her outstanding soccer abilities, questions started to circulate about her sexual identity. Instead of focusing on a player's skill and talent, many media outlets try to understand or explain why the athlete differs so greatly from traditional standards of femininity.

Many female athletes competing in those sports commonly viewed as "masculine," such as boxing, ice hockey, and soccer, or those who have wrongly been associated with primarily lesbian participation, such as softball and basketball, find they must conform to traditional stereotypes associated with women to avoid having their sexual identities questioned and examined. Many female athletes, to avoid being mislabeled or having assumptions made about them, will manage their appearance so that they look more stereotypically feminine. They will wear skirts and high heels, put on makeup, and style their hair to fight the perception that they are gay. This form of discrimination is called heterosexism.

Heterosexism is a form of discrimination that favors people who are straight over those who are gay. It affects women regardless of their actual sexual orientation. Many gay athletes are hesitant to come out publicly for fear that they will be discriminated against or lose the support of fans, teammates, coaches, and sponsors. Athletes who are straight, but whose sexuality may be questioned because of their athletic ability or the assumptions made about their sport, often overcompensate and try to appear "hyper-feminine" in an effort to dispel any doubt about their sexual identity.

#COVERTHEATHLETE

During the 2016 Summer Olympics in Rio de Janeiro, Brazil, swimming fans were outraged by a headline published by the *Bryan-College Station Eagle*. In large font, the headline read: "Phelps ties for silver in 100 fly," referencing decorated swimmer Michael Phelp's silver medal win. However, in a smaller font underneath, a sub-heading read: "Ledecky sets world record in women's 800 freestyle," for Katie Ledecky's world record in the prestigious 800-meter freestyle race. With this win, Ledecky became the first woman to win gold in the 200-, 400-, and 800-meter freestyle races since swimmer Debbie Mayer in 1968. In response to this stilted headline, a photo of the article in question went viral with thousands of fans asking why Ledecky's achievements seemed less worthy of attention than Phelp's. Largely in response to media bias like this, social media users have coined the hashtag #CovertheAthlete to encourage journalists to fairly and accurately cover female athletes.

Swimmer Katie Ledecky is one of the fastest swimmers in the world and returned home from the 2016 Summer Olympics with five Olympic medals.

EMBRACING MEDIA ATTENTION

Some female athletes fight the media's gender-stereotyped coverage of them. They argue that, by portraying female athletes either as sexy or beautiful, the media is spreading a message that says women are not as skilled, strong, powerful, or capable as male athletes. Other female athletes, however, embrace the way the media covers them and use it to their advantage. They are challenging the assumption that sexy images undermine the importance and validity of women's athletics. These athletes are savvy about marketing and understand how creating and managing their own images can bring more attention to their athletic abilities and increase their overall popularity.

From 2007 until 2016, GoDaddy.com—a company that registers internet domain names—sponsored Danica Patrick's racing team. Patrick is the first female driver to win an Indy Car race. In television ads for GoDaddy, she would often appear in a bikini wearing four-inch heels. Patrick doesn't shy away from using her appearance to garner attention, nor does she apologize for it. She uses the fact that she's an attractive woman to her advantage. Patrick told the *New York Times*, "I'm a girl, and so to say I can't use being a girl doesn't make any sense. In this world, there's so much competition out there that you have to use everything that you have to make sponsors happy, to attract them, to be unique, to be different."

Patrick has embraced what makes her unique in a sport dominated by men. She knows how to market herself and has used the media to her advantage. As a result she is one of the most recognizable names in racing. According to Nielsen/E-Poll N-Score, which tracks the public's awareness of individual athletes, 30 percent of the population knows who Patrick is. The average male racecar driver is known by only 9 percent of the population, as are most female athletes. Patrick has also brought more attention and viewers to her sport. In 2013, according to *Sports Illustrated*, there was a 24 percent higher television viewing audience than in previous years for the Daytona 500 race in which she participated.

Another sports star who has capitalized both on her skills and appearance to raise awareness of women in professional sports is Alex Morgan. Morgan played on both the Olympic and World Cup teams for US women's soccer. She scored the game-winning goal in the 2012 London Olympics and has been named US Soccer Female Athlete of the Year and Fédération Internationale de Football Association (FIFA) World Player of the Year. Morgan has also appeared in the *Sports Illustrated* Swimsuit issued and on the cover of many national magazines, including *Shape, Vogue,* and *Elle*. Her endorsement deals and media literacy have made her one of the most highly paid athletes in the world. In 2015, FIFA, the international governing association of soccer, published a profile of Morgan on their website that stated: "Alex Morgan is one of the most popular players in USA women's football. A talented goalscorer with a style that is very easy on the eye and good looks to match, she is nothing short of a media phenomenon." This description drew wide criticism from the public due to its focus on Morgan's looks instead of her achievements in soccer.

Patrick and Morgan's acceptance of the ways in which media covers women's sports, and their skill at taking advantage of society's need to view women as attractive and feminine, raises an important question: Why do women have to choose between being athletic and being beautiful or feminine? Does a sexy image of a female athlete have to be inherently demeaning? Women should not have to choose between being athletic and being feminine. They can embrace their athletic accomplishments and celebrate their femininity without feeling as if doing so is personally degrading or in some way damaging to women's athletics as a whole.

Patrick, Morgan, and other athletes, such as gymnast Aly Raisman, tennis player Caroline Wozniacki, and Olympic swimmer Natalie Coughlin have all actively participated in photo shoots and marketing campaigns that flaunt their beauty. This approach, as Patrick and Morgan have proven, can attract more attention to a female competitor than her strictly athletic accomplishments.

FIGHTING FOR EQUAL RIGHTS

Since their beginning in ancient Greece, the Olympic Games have grown to be one of the most important sporting events in the world. However, women were not allowed to participate in the ancient Olympic Games and achieving gender equality since then has taken quite some time. Only since 2012 have women competed in all sporting events in this prestigious and international competition. Since 1991, new sports that entered into the Olympics program were required to have both male and female teams. Outside of the Olympic arena, equality for female athletes was harder to come by. While

Female athletes, activists, and celebrities have advocated for Title IX, including (*from left to right*) soccer player Julie Foudy, senator Patty Murray, gymnast Dominique Dawes, and actresses Holly Hunter and Geena Davis.

women have always participated in sports and sporting events, organized, competitive athletics didn't become a reality in the United States until the passing of federal legislation that required equality for female athletes.

TITLE IX

The Civil Rights Act of 1964 was written to end discrimination based on race, color, or national origin. The passage of this bill energized women to push for more gender equality and better defined women's rights. Congresswomen Patsy Mink, who wrote the legislation for Title IX, originally focused on the hiring and employment practices of federally financed institutions. Her goal was to ensure women were treated equally to men in all hiring practices.

While Title IX doesn't mention sports specifically in its legislation, it does provide overriding protection from discrimination based on sex in educational programs and activities that receive money from the federal government. Title IX ensures that:

- Women and men are given equal opportunities to participate in sports. Female and male student-athletes receive athletic scholarship dollars proportional to their participation in sports.
- Female and male student-athletes are provided for equally when in comes to sporting equipment; scheduling of games and practices times; travel; coaching; athletic, training, and housing facilities; medical and training staff; support services; and recruiting.

When President Richard Nixon signed the act on July 23, 1972, only about 31,000 women were involved in college sports at the time. Less than $100,000 was spent on athletic scholarships for women and colleges had less than half the number of women's teams as they did men's teams.

Several organizations fought against the mandates of Title IX, including the National Collegiate Athletic Association (NCAA), which tried to block the legislation in the 1970s and 1980s. Some colleges cut men's athletic programs in order to comply with Title IX. Several male athletes sued over program cuts, and some female athletes were blamed for the colleges' decisions. A key argument made against Title IX was that it appeared to inspire gender discrimination against men.

In 2000, President George W. Bush called for a reexamination of Title IX. He issued revised guidelines that inserted loopholes in the legislation that made it easier for colleges and universities to avoid their obligation to provide equal opportunities to female athletes. President Barack Obama reversed Bush's weakening of Title IX and fully restored the original legislation. After considerable lobbying by women's groups, laws were put in place to punish those who did not comply with Title IX.

THE BENEFITS OF TITLE IX

Just six years after Title IX was passed, the percentage of girls playing team sports jumped from 4 percent to 25 percent. In 1972, close to 30,000 women were competing in NCAA-sponsored sports. Today, there are more than 160,000 female student-athletes competing in college sports. The impact of Title IX reaches far beyond sports. The increase in girls' athletic participation was associated with a 7 percent lower risk of obesity twenty to twenty-five years later, when this first generation of Title IX girls were women in their late thirties and early forties.

There are incredible benefits to playing sports for girls. In addition to making friends, having fun, and learning new skills like teamwork and leadership, athletics impact girls' lives in valuable ways:

- **Empowerment**: Female athletes are more confident and have better self-esteem. They also have a more positive body image than those who don't play sports.
- **Better Grades**: Being involved in sports helps girls do better in school. Exercise helps improve memory and concentration, which helps students learn more effectively. Sports also require students to manage their time. Those involved in a number of activities, including sports, tend to be more efficient with time management and schedule juggling.
- **Teamwork and Goal-Setting Skills**: Learning to be a team player is an important lesson.

Later in life, when women get jobs, they will work with a variety of different personalities. Learning to work together to solve problems and meet goals is essential for success both on and off the field.

- **Health Benefits:** In addition to being fit and maintaining a healthy weight, athletes are less likely to smoke, have a lower risk of getting certain cancers, including breast cancer, and reduced incidence of other illnesses, such as osteoporosis, later in life. Girls who are athletic often are at a healthier weight and have a reduced risk of becoming obese. They have better blood pressure and blood sugar levels and lower cholesterol.

- **Manage Stress and Pressure**: It can be stressful to manage your studies, a part-time job, family commitments, and friendships. Sports help to diffuse stress and give you an outlet to work off anxiety and pressure. Physical activity is a natural mood lifter and helps to fight depression. Having teammates who share the same experience can also help you feel like you have a built-in support group that understands what you are going through.

- **General Wellness:** Girls who play sports report feeling happier than those who don't participate in athletics. They often have more energy and enjoy a better overall quality of life.

FIGHTING FOR EQUAL FOOTING

Title IX tried to provide equality for women's sports in high schools and college, but the federal legislation did not impact sporting events held outside of the confines of academic institutions. Women still had to fight for participation in a number of sporting events not sponsored by or organized under the auspices of academia.

Kathrine Switzer, the first woman to officially register and compete in the Boston Marathon, did so

A race official attempts to force Kathrine Switzer off the Boston Marathon course in 1967. Switzer was the first woman to officially register and compete in the race.

under false pretenses in 1967. At the time, women were not allowed to race in the Boston Marathon, so Switzer registered under "K. Switzer." While running, Switzer was nearly forced off the course by Jock Semple, a race official who tried to tear off her race number and physically remove her from competition. Switzer's then-boyfriend blocked Semple, and Switzer finished the race. Switzer's extraordinary effort sparked an interest in women's running. She continued to compete in races, winning the 1974 New York City Marathon.

Switzer has dedicated her career to creating opportunities and equal sport status for women. She created the a series of international running events for women in more than twenty-five countries. Her support and advocacy for women's running led to the inclusion of the women's marathon in the Olympic Games.

PAY DISPARITY

While Title IX has helped to level the playing field for women to participate in athletics, it hasn't helped to equalize the earnings or salaries of professional female athletes and coaches with those of their male counterparts. Prize money is much less for women than men in nearly all sports. Take professional golf, for example: the winner of the US Women's Golf Open in 2015 won $810,000, compared to $1.8 million that was awarded to male winner of the US Open. For a

Golfer In Gee Chun, winner of the US Women's Open
in 2015, won significantly less money than her

WNBA player with a minimum of three years in the league, the minimum salary is $54,000. For NBA players, the minimum salary for a first year player is more than $473,000.

Very few sporting events award equal prize money to men and women. For winning the 2015 Women's World Cup, the US women's national soccer team was awarded $2 million; however, when the men's team left the World Cup before the quarterfinals, they were paid $9 million. Because of this pay discrepancy, five players from the US women's national team filed a lawsuit accusing the US Soccer Federation for gender-based wage discrimination. In April 2017, the team signed a new collective bargaining agreement with US Soccer that raised players' pay, though they still make less than the male players. Other important steps have been taken in recent years to combat gender-based pay discrepancies. In 2007, the Championships, Wimbledon announced for the first time that the tournament would award equal prize purses to male and female tennis players. All four Grand Slam events now offer equal prize money to the champions.

The pay inequity affects coaches as well. Female head coaches of Division I teams received an average salary of $850,400, while head coaches for men's teams average $1,783,100.

MYTHS AND
FACTS

There are many myths about women in sports, particularly regarding women's physical abilities and past accomplishments. Here are three of the most common myths you might hear, along with the facts that refute these claims:

MYTH: Women are physically weaker and slower than men and, thus, will never be as good in sports as men.

FACT: Athletic ability largely depends on an individual and is not necessarily dictated by gender. Women are typically smaller in stature than men, which means that the average woman does not have the same muscle mass or strength as the average man. However, there are varying degrees of strength and size among men and women. Also, on average, women tend to be more flexible than men and have a greater percentage of body fat, which makes women particularly good at sports like marathon swimming and long-distance running.

MYTH: Women are not as interested in sports as men, so reaching gender equality in college sports will never happen.

FACT: While most colleges have more male athletes than female athletes, this is largely due to discrepancies in recruitment. On average, colleges pay $139,000 in recruitment for men's sports and only $28,840 for women's sports. If equal money was spent on recruitment for both male

(continued on the next page)

(continued from the previous page)

MYTHS AND
FACTS

and female athletes, many more female athletes would participate in college sports.

MYTH: Title IX has led to fewer opportunities for men in sports.

FACT: Compliance with Title IX has not led to fewer opportunities for men in high school and college sports. While it has led to more opportunities for female athletes, these female athletes have not displaced male athletes. In fact, athletic opportunities for both men and women have increased since the passage of Title IX.

EXTREME MEASURES

In the 1980s, Christy Henrich was young and had her whole career as a professional gymnast ahead of her. She made the US national gymnastics team at the age of fourteen and later won a silver medal in the US National Championships. She aspired to become an Olympic athlete and placed ninth in the 1988 Olympic Trials, which was a solid ranking. But then, after a meet, Henrich received some negative feedback during a critique session with a US judge, who suggested she was "too fat" to make the Olympic team.

Devastated by the comment, Henrich focused on losing weight while she trained for the Olympics. She weighed just 90 pounds (41 kg) when she competed for a spot on

Female athletes in such sports as gymnastics, which places greater emphasis on the physical appearance of competitors, are more likely to have eating disorders than

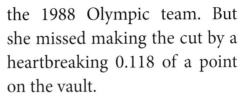

the 1988 Olympic team. But she missed making the cut by a heartbreaking 0.118 of a point on the vault.

Henrich's eating disorder, anorexia nervosa, is a condition in which one severely limits the amount of calories she consumes. Henrich once commented that she could survive on just three apples a day. Henrich's illness took such a toll that she was forced to retire from gymnastics after repeated hospitalizations. At twenty-two years old, Henrich died from multiple organ failure. She weighed only 47 pounds (21 kg) at the time of her death.

Henrich took extreme measures in her attempt to attain her goals. Yet it's not uncommon for female athletes to have disturbed eating patterns, develop full-blown eating disorders, or take steroids to control their appearance or enhance their performance.

DYING FOR PERFECTION

Gymnast Cathy Rigby was instructed by her coaches not to weight more than 85 pounds (39 kg). The gymnast, who in the 1960s and 1970s won twelve international medals over the course of her career, suffered from bulimia for years. Rigby almost died twice after suffering from cardiac arrest because of an electrolyte imbalance caused by her eating disorder. Even after retiring, Rigby continued to battle bulimia.

According to two studies of college athletes conducted by eating disorder experts, at least one-third of all female athletes exhibit some level of disordered eating. This can range from constant dieting and taking laxatives and diet pills to the occasional binge eating and purging. Some athletes become so obsessive about their weight that they develop serious eating disorders, like anorexia nervosa or bulimia nervosa.

For female athletes, athletic ability and appearance are judged hand-in-hand. Because of this added emphasis on physical beauty, rather than just physical ability, eating disorders are a common and serious issue amongst female athletes. Certain sports, such as gymnastics, diving, dance, and figure skating, have a judging system that is subjective. This puts pressure on an athlete to be not only be athletic and powerful, but also to be thin and pretty even though one's looks have no effect on one's physical performance.

Swimmer and Olympic gold medalist Amanda Beard has

Seven-time Olympic gold medalist Amanda Beard has struggled with an eating disorder since she was a teenager. At the 1996 Olympics, at just fourteen years old, Beard became the second-youngest Olympic medalist in American swimming history when she won three gold and two silver medals. The next year, a normal growth spurt added eight inches (20 cm) and 25 pounds (11 kg) to Beard's body. After performing poorly at a swim invitational, Beard read newspaper articles predicting the demise of her career and calling her Olympic victories a fluke. Beard began struggling with body issues and developed an eating disorder. At its worse, she would force herself to throw up six to seven times a day.

Henrich and Beard's stories are common for women in sports. Women athletes experience an immense pressure to be thin and to maintain a certain body weight or shape. The prevalence of eating disorders among female athletes competing in sports in which aesthetics are important—such as figure skating and gymnastics—is significantly higher than female athletes who participate in non-aesthetic or non-weight-dependent sports, such as weight lifting, soccer, or volleyball.

Henrich's eating disorder, anorexia nervosa, is characterized by an obsessive fear of gaining weight. People with anorexia nervosa feel hungry, but deny themselves full meals. Instead, they allow themselves to eat only very small amounts of food. Anorexia nervosa is a serious mental illness. It can lead to hair loss, depression, a distorted self-image, bad breath, general poor health, malnutrition, heart disease, and in extreme cases, like Henrich's, death from organ failure due to starvation.

Beard's disorder, bulimia nervosa is an illness in which a person binge eats, or eats excessive amounts of food, then purges the food they just ate by forcing themselves to vomit. Bulimia sufferers also abuse laxatives, use diuretics, or engage in excessive exercise. Bulimia nervosa is nine times more likely to occur in women than men and can lead to serious health issues such as infertility, chronic gastric reflux, constipation, and an electrolyte imbalance, which can lead to cardiac arrhythmia, cardiac arrest, and even death.

FOOD AS FUEL

A healthy athlete knows that food is fuel for her body. Muscles need protein, and carbohydrates give an athlete the energy to compete hard. However, an athlete with a distorted view of food and eating doesn't see food as a source of energy and fuel. Instead, they view food simply in terms of unwanted calories and fat.

Eating disorders are found in all sports and can afflict men as well as women. But for athletes participating in activities that emphasize a thin, slender body for optimal performance, such as figure skating, gymnastics, and swimming, the risk for developing an eating disorder is significantly greater. A cross-country runner might seek to control her weight by eating less. She thinks this will make her lighter and faster. A gymnast might want to lose weight because she thinks judges are looking at her size and shape as well as her ability. She believes that being thinner might improve her scores.

Obsessively counting calories and restricting food intake wreaks havoc on an athlete's body and will affect her performance. The body needs food for energy as well as muscle growth and regeneration. Without energy and nutrients, the body can't perform as well, endurance suffers, and muscle strength and the immune system weaken.

Even the biggest names in women's athletics are not free of the pressure to achieve a particular look. Nadia Comaneci, the nine-time Olympic Gold medalist in gymnastics, admitted to suffering from both anorexia and bulimia. Nancy Kerrigan, a two-time Olympic medalist in figure skating, has also struggled with an eating disorder.

PERFORMANCE-ENHANCING DRUGS

Marion Jones was at one time considered one of the greatest female athletes in history. She was the fastest female runner in the world, with world records in

Olympic runner Marion Jones was stripped of many of her titles when it was discovered she had used performance-the 100- and 200-meter events. Her successful quest to become the first female athlete to win five medals in track and field in one Olympics at the 2000 Sydney games was followed by news organizations and awe-struck viewers around the world.

A year after her historic Olympic performance, however, Jones was suspected of using performance-enhancing drugs (PEDs). It would take six more years for Jones to admit to using steroids, which she told investigators she began using in 1999. Jones was stripped of her Olympic medals and sent to prison for six months after pleading guilty to lying to investigators about her use of steroids. It was a sad end to a career that was watched by millions of people around the world and, in particular, by young girls everywhere who were inspired by Jones to become athletes themselves.

Steroid use by athletes is a dark secret in sports. Steroids are synthetic hormones that help the body produce muscle and help muscles recover faster from tough workouts. They can lessen or prevent muscle breakdown and increase the level of testosterone in the body. Testosterone is a hormone that stimulates muscle tissue to grow bigger and stronger. Some steroid medications are legal, but these are only available with a doctor's prescription. Obtaining them in any other way is against the law.

Athletes use steroids for a number of reasons. Steroids can help muscles become more defined and stronger. They can boost self-esteem and confidence. They can help athletes perform more effectively. Steroids can also reduce the recovery time that muscles require after workouts or competition. But steroids are unhealthy and even dangerous. For women, the side effects can be drastic. Female athletes who take steroids experience a deepening of their voice, hair loss, aggressive behavior, mood swings, and depression. They lose the natural curves that are typically associated with a women's body, and their breasts can shrink in size. Many women's bodies will become more masculine looking on steriods.

Steroid use has extremely negative repercussions for the body and these harmful effects can last for years, even long after consumption stops. The liver and heart can be damaged permanently. In addition, reproductive disorders and other illnesses, such as diabetes, can occur later in life as a result of steroid abuse, long after an athlete has stopped competing.

Aside from the physical impact steroids have on a woman's body, steroids are illegal. For athletes found using them, the penalties are steep. Professional and college athletes are regularly drug tested. A woman who fails a drug test can be kicked off her team and forced to forfeit any awards or trophies she has earned. She can also face serious legal actions, fines, and even jail time

THE GENDER BREAKDOWN OF DOPING VIOLATIONS

In January 2016, the World Anti-Doping Agency released data showing that more than four times as many male professional athletes have tested positive

Rita Jeptoo, one of the fastest women in the world, was also stripped of several titles for using PEDs.

for performance-enhancing drugs than female professional athletes. However, this doesn't mean that female athletes are less likely to dope. Rather, the difference is most likely due to the fact that women are not tested as often for PEDs as men are. Since women are perceived as less likely to use such drugs, they are tested less often than men. This perception is based on gender stereotypes, however, and is not rooted in fact. In recent years, some high-profile female athletes, including the marathoner Rita Jeptoo, have tested positive for using PEDs. According to Annie Skinner, a spokeswoman for the United States Anti-Doping Association, "We know that the win-at-all costs culture exists in all sports, at all levels, and that the temptation to use performance-enhancing drugs to cheat your competitor isn't limited by gender."

STEROID USE

Steroids aren't found just in the locker rooms of professional athletes. They are also present in high schools and colleges and are used by teens as young as thirteen to help influence their athletic performance. A study in 2008 surveyed students in grades 8 through 12. Of those who admitted using steroids, 57 percent said steroid use among professional athletes influenced their decision. Eighty percent of these teen steroid users said they believed steroids could help them achieve their athletic dreams and that they were willing to take the risks associated with steroid use if it meant they could reach the professional level of competition.

Even though teens know the physical harm that steroids can cause, many still don't see anything wrong with using them. And while a number of athletes in recent years have been involved in steroid scandals—from more than eighty major league baseball stars to players on the North Korean women's World Cup soccer team—most teens still believe it should be a professional athlete's right to use steroids if they choose.

While steroids are illegal, there are a number of performance enhancing supplements, such as protein powders, creatine, and amino acids, that can be used to build body mass. Other supplements, such as pills that encourage the burning of fat, high-energy drinks, ephedra, and caffeine pills are used to control weight. While legal, none of these supplements are healthy and abuse of them is dangerous.

WOMEN, CULTURE, AND SPORTS

Lindsey Vonn is one of the most famous—as well as one of the modest decorated—alpine skiers in the world. She won a gold medal at the 2010 Vancouver Winter Olympics and has won seventy-seven World Cup races. She is one of only two female skiers to have ever won four World Cup championships and holds the record for all-time World Cup victories. In 2010, the US Olympic Committee named Vonn Sportswoman of the Year. Without a doubt, Vonn is one of the most successful American skiers in history.

Media coverage followed her success at the Olympics, including the cover of *Sports Illustrated*. Yet instead of featuring an action shot of Vonn skiing down a mountain, emphasizing

Lindsey Vonn is one of the most decorated alpine skiers of all times, yet the media often focuses on her physical appearance rather than on her athletic abilities.

her athletic talent, the magazine portrayed Vonn in a suggestive position on its cover. This was yet another example of how female athletes are significantly more likely to be portrayed in ways that emphasize their femininity and heterosexuality rather than their athletic prowess.

Tennis star Roger Federer has won a record eighteen Grand Slam singles titles. On a cover of *Sports Illustrated*, a photo of Federer highlights his power and strength as he stands ready to strike a tennis ball. Anna Kournikova, one of the best-known female tennis players in the world, was also featured on a cover of *Sports Illustrated*. She, however, was portrayed first and foremost as an attractive, sexy woman instead of a powerful athlete. Kournikova was photographed with her long blond hair down and styled, wearing a pink blouse, and lying on a pillow.

FEMALE ATHLETES IN THE MEDIA

Men's sports and male athletes are predominately featured on sports networks like ESPN, in advertisements for products, and on magazine covers in ways that emphasize their athletic ability and achievements. In contrast, female athletes are portrayed as sexy instead of athletic and powerful. Study after study has revealed that newspaper and television coverage around the globe routinely focuses on the purely athletic exploits

Anna Kournikova (*left*) and Lindsay Davenport (*right*) speak during a doubles match. Davenport won more titles during her career but received less media attention.

of male competitors while offering hyper-sexualized images of their female counterparts. Media images that focus on femininity or sexuality disrespect female athletes and places a greater—and highly irrelevant—emphasis on looks rather than athletic ability.

Even among female athletes, looks, not athletic ability, seem to for count more. Tennis player Lindsay Davenport won thirty-eight career titles and was ranked number one in both women's singles and doubles. Fellow tennis star Anna Kournikova never won a major tournament. Yet Kournikova is more widely known by the general public than Davenport and has received many major endorsement deals, largely because of her perceived attractiveness and femininity.

A LACK OF COVERAGE

Every five years, since 1989, a study is conducted that analyzes the amount and type of coverage women's sports receive by sports media outlets such as ESPN. Although 40 percent of all athletes are female, researchers found that only between two and four percent of sports media coverage is devoted to women's sports. They also found that the type of coverage women's sports received was less about outstanding play, individual achievements, or team accomplishments, and more about specific incidents in women's sports, such as hair pulling during a soccer game. The study's results support an argument media scholars have been making for years: a consequence of the media's tendency to present female athletes as sexy and attractive, focusing

NATIONAL GIRLS AND WOMEN IN SPORTS DAY

For over thirty-one years, National Girls and Women in Sports Day (NGWSD) has been held on February 1. The day celebrates the passage of Title IX and aims to bring attention to the continued need for access to sports for women and girls.

Begun in 1987, NGWSD was first marked by special women's sports events around Washington, DC. The first NGWSD was also held in remembrance of Olympic volleyball player Flo Hyman, who dedicated her life to her sport and to women's equality in sports. Today, it is celebrated around the United States through community-based events, award ceremonies, and other celebrations. Accomplished athletes such as skier and six-time Winter X Games medalist Grete Eliassen, soccer player and two-time Olympic gold medalist Angela Hucles, and softball player and National Collegiate Athletic Association (NCAA) All-Time Home Run Record Holder Lauren Chamberlain, all participated in NGWSD events in 2017.

less on their athletic ability and accomplishments, reinforces the idea that women's sports are second-rate and therefore not worthy of being as respected as men's sports.

It's not that women's sports fail to find an audience. Each year during the NCAA's March Madness tournament, women's college basketball games have record attendance and high TV ratings. The coverage highlights the long-standing traditions of some of the college teams, conference rivals, and legendary coaches. Women's World Cup soccer also consistently receives strong TV ratings. The 2015 World Cup final between the United States and Japan was the most-watched soccer match in US history with approximately 23 million viewers in the United States and 750 million viewers worldwide. Both these events showcase strong, athletic women exhibiting great skill in their respective sports.

But those responsible for promoting women's sports, mainly journalists, marketing professionals, and advertisers, take a different approach. They see the depiction of female athletes as feminine and attractive as the best strategy for selling women's sports to a mainly male television audience.

Female athletes claim national and world titles in a number of sports and win gold, silver, and bronze medals at the Olympics year after year. But more and more, media images of female athletes cast them in

Swimmer Dara Torres was featured in a skimpy bikini as part of the "Got Milk?" advertising campaign, while male athletes were shown fully dressed.

overly feminine roles or hyper-sexualized roles. Since 2009, *ESPN The Magazine* has published the so-called "Body Issue," in which professional athletes pose nude and semi-nude. While both male and female athletes are featured in its pages, the female athletes are showcased and receive the most attention. For example, a 2009 "Got Milk?" advertisement showed decorated swimmer Dara Torres in a skimpy bikini with a suggestive tag line. Similar "Got Milk?" advertisements showed male athletes fully dressed and posing with their sports equipment or in the middle of an action shot. Images of female athletes tend to be either non-threatening to men or overly sexualized. Studies show that men see high performing women as a threat to the traditional male dominance of sports.

LATINA ATHLETES

National studies show that Hispanic girls have some of the lowest percentages of participation in sports. Unique cultural pressures often influence their interest in and ability to take part in athletics. In Latino culture, families often have old-fashioned views concerning the proper roles of men and women. Traditionally, Latina girls often help out with family obligations after school, whether watching younger siblings or pitching in around the house with chores or preparing dinner while their parents are working. These responsibilities leave little time for sports, or make it hard for a girl to make a commitment to a sports team when she can't be at practice on a regular basis.

Sports are also not seen as a priority in many Latino families. Social pressures and ethnic and cultural traditions often shape girls' attitudes about femininity, competition, and aggression. These attitudes can sometimes serve to discourage Hispanic girls from playing sports. Other factors, including poverty and language barriers, also keep Latina girls away from sports. The strong Latino emphasis on education as the primary pathway to success also accounts for lower numbers of female Latina athletes. But in recent years, those roles have been changing, and Latino families are seeing the benefits that playing sports can have for their daughters.

Historically, there have been very few role models for Latina girls to emulate, though there have been some very successful Latina athletes. These include Lisa Fernandez, a pitcher for the US national softball team, who won Olympic gold medals in 1996, 2000, and 2004; Nancy Lopez, who won forty-eight golf tournaments, including three majors; and Mary Joe Fernández, who won two Olympic Gold medals in doubles tennis. Yet the number of Latina professional athletes is few.

In recent years, many leading Latino magazines have begun to feature Latina athletes on their covers

AMY RODRIGUEZ

Soccer player Amy Rodriguez, known as "A Rod" by her fans, was the only Latina on the 2015 US women's World Cup roster. Born to a Cuban-American father, Rodriguez is proud of her Latin American roots and has stated that she was "surprised" to be the only Latina picked for the US Women's World Cup team. In an interview with Fox News, she stated that there were a lot of Latina soccer players with great potential and that she hoped her success in soccer would inspire young girls who might otherwise be discouraged to pursue professional sports. "I think [the inclusion of Latinas in professional soccer] will change in the future," she said.

Rodriguez is also inspirational to female athletes for another reason. After taking 2013 off from professional soccer in order to have her son, she trained hard to make the World Cup roster in 2015. Rodriguez spent many hours each week working with fitness trainers and a support team to get back to her prior fitness level after giving birth. Rodriguez showed the world that a woman who had recently given birth could compete with other athletes and win a prestigious spot on the World Cup team,

(continued on the next page)

(continued from the previous page)

proving that a woman's decision to become a mother does not mean that she will no longer be competitive in professional sports.

Soccer player Amy Rodriguez was the only Latina on the US women's World Cup roster in 2015.

to bring more attention to the benefits of sports for girls and to provide strong role models. *Latina*, a health, beauty, and fashion magazine, has featured profiles of US Women's soccer player Amy Rodriguez, professional golfer Lorena Ochoa, and Jennifer Rodriguez, a two-time bronze medalist in speed skating at the 2002 Winter Olympics and the first Cuban-American to compete and medal in a Winter Olympics.

Sports's positive effects are helping to introduce more Latina girls to athletics. Parents, who were previously reluctant to encourage their daughters to join sports teams, now see sports as a way to keep their children out of trouble, get better grades, and graduate from high school. Studies have shown that Hispanic girls are at greater risk than non-Hispanic peers for teen pregnancy and obesity and are more likely to drop out of school. Sports are helping to reverse these trends.

BLACK FEMALE ATHLETES

While women in general fight for equality in sports, black female athletes face additional hurdles in their quest for equality and respect. Black female athletes face an even greater level of discrimination and negative stereotyping by fans and the media. They also face barriers to athletic involvement that include limited access to quality coaching and training; the high cost

of equipment or participation; and pressure from peers to quit.

Often, fans and the media define black female athletes as too aggressive, too strong, too athletic, or too masculine. Rarely are black female athletes described in more complementary ways. An example of this is the coverage of black gymnast Gabby Douglas. In 2012, Gabby Douglas became the first African-American woman to become the Olympic individual all-around champion at the London Olympic Games. However, following her win, she faced harsh media criticism for not appearing happy in photos when her teammates' won competitions and for not placing her hand over her heart during the medal ceremony. In 2016, during the Rio Olympic Games, Douglas was the subject of insults on social media because she wore her hair in its natural texture during the competition. Of course, Douglas's hair has nothing to do with her athletic performance.

The Williams Sisters, Venus and Serena, have also consistently faced negativity and harsh criticism in spite of their domination in women's tennis. At the Wimbledon tournament, they were consistently scheduled to play on Court 2, not Court 1, the tennis center's main, larger venue. During the 2009 Australian Open final, ESPN tennis commentator Mary Carillo criticized Serena Williams's commitment to the game. At the Australian Open, both sisters were left off of the tournament's list of "beautiful women of tennis." Dominating the list were slender, white European tennis players.

The Williams' sisters, despite their Grand Slam titles and No. 1 rankings, have been unable to redefine society's view of how a female athlete should look. Black female athletes face this challenge consistently. Muscular, strong, athletic women like the Williams sisters are often on the receiving side of one recurring insult. They are told: "You look like a man."

Black women represent a very low percentage of athletes in high school and college. Less than 5 percent of all high school athletes and less than 10 percent of all college athletes are black women. They most often get involved in basketball, track and field, and other sports that have fewer costs for participation. There are very few black gymnasts, figure skaters, tennis players, and soccer players. The twenty-three-player roster of the women's 2015 US World Cup team had only one

Latina athlete. There were no African-Americans or Asian-Americans on the team.

A reason for this gap in diversity in many sports is access. Golf, tennis, and swimming do not have youth programs that can serve as a pipeline to high school and college sports teams. Gymnastics, tennis, and figure skating all require extensive coaching and access to equipment not commonly found in high schools or community centers. By comparison, basketball and track and field are less expensive sports that offer easy access. In these sports, raw talent can be developed with less specialized and knowledgeable coaching. Even soccer leagues can have expensive registration fees and travel expenses that deter parents with a lower income from enrolling their children. This helps to explain why participation by young black girls is low in some sports, but high in others.

CHAPTER 6

JUGGLING SPORTS AND LIFE

Professional golfer Michelle Wie has spent most of her life balancing the demands of professional golf with her education and her personal life. At the age of ten, Wie became the youngest golfer ever to qualify to play in the prestigious United States Golf Association (USGA) amateur championship. Wie turned professional shortly after her sixteenth birthday. She placed in several prestigious competitions on the LPGA Tour while a student at Stanford University. Wie would often spend late nights studying while preparing for golf competitions. In 2012, after years of hard work, Wie graduated from Stanford with a degree in communications.

Golfer Michelle Wie spent many years juggling her education and her personal life with her professional golf career.

BALANCING IT ALL

Wie's life of juggling college classes and golf tournaments, coursework and travel, is a common balancing act for a student-athlete. Wie understood from a young age that her golf career wouldn't last forever and that she would need something to fall back on. Her communications degree will open doors for her to continue to be involved in the world of golf (and sports in general) as a commentator or sports anchor after retiring from the sport—if she chooses. In the meantime, however, Wie continues to take the golf world by storm and has won four major golf championships, including first place in the 2014 US Women's Open.

Wie's course work has given her something else to focus on besides golf. She chose to go to college to fulfill a personal goal, but attending school also provided her with an alternative existence when the pressures of playing professional golf get to be too much. When Wie sustained an injury that sidelined her from play, she concentrated on her studies and not on the tournaments she was missing. She also credits school with slowing down her golf career, which has helped her avoid getting burned out—a common problem for young professional athletes. Most importantly, college gave Wie a chance to enjoy all the things that ordinary twenty-somethings do and experience.

As many student-athletes will attest, playing sports, at both the high school and college levels, is a time consuming commitment. Athletes practice five-to-six days a week and travel for games. They attend classes and spend much of their time off the practice field studying and working on homework assignments

When deciding where to go to college, particularly as a student-athlete, it is important to speak with an academic adviser to learn what will be expected from you as both a student and an athlete. Here are ten great questions to ask during an appointment with a college advisor:

1. What position do you want me to play and how many other students are you recruiting for the same position?

2. What are the academic performance requirements to remain a student-athlete?

3. What is the graduation rate among student-athletes?

4. How long does it typically take for an athlete like me to graduate from your school?

5. Has drug use been an issue either at your school or in your athletic program?

6. What kinds of athletic scholarships are available?

7. What will happen to my scholarship if I become injured?

8. What is required of me to maintain my athletic scholarship?

9. How much time per week is required for practice?

10. What will be expected of me during the off-season?

and class projects. They receive no extra time to complete class assignments and must participate in coursework just like everyone else. Each student-athlete is required to earn a minimum number of credits toward graduation each semester, and failing to keep up with their academics has negative implications for their athletic activities. Failing to maintain a minimum grade point average puts their athletic eligibility at risk.

Maintaining such a full schedule of athletic and academic commitments has an impact on other aspects of a student's college experience. Student-athletes often do not have time to participate in other campus activities, such as clubs or organizations. Holding down a part-time job can be difficult when free time is limited and a full schedule of practices and games cuts into one's availability for work shifts.

Student-athletes face difficult decisions when they are offered academic opportunities that conflict with their athletic ambitions. Some athletes have given up prestigious fellowships and research grants because they would interfere with athletic pursuits by creating management problems and scheduling conflicts. For college athletes, commitment to the team and to their own long-term plans for a career are often at odds. Scholarships give students a chance to continue to play sports in college while providing financial support for their education. But scholarships are contracts that require students to attend all

Members of the University of California, Los Angeles, golfing team pose on campus with their clubs.

practices and games, while also maintaining a certain grade point average.

For many women, college athletics are both the high point and the conclusion of their sports careers. Since there are so few professional sports leagues for women, the vast majority of female college athletes will not play professional sports once they graduate. Their studies are important because their academic degrees will earn them a job once they complete college. Passing up a fellowship or research opportunity could hurt their long-term career goals.

While a full schedule of course work, homework, projects, exams, practice, travel, and games can encourage the development of strong time management skills in student-athletes, it can also lead to stress and pressure. Some college academic advisors often tell student-athletes to choose less demanding majors if they want to play sports or if they are on a sports scholarship. While choosing a program of study with a lesser workload can help students manage their time better, this may not be the best advice for athletes on a scholarship. Many student-athletes could not afford to attend college without their scholarships. They may have been recruited to play sports for a college, but the education they receive in the classroom will have a far more enduring value—including monetary value—than the time they spend on the court or playing field.

ANXIETY AND DEPRESSION

The pressure to balance athletic commitments with schoolwork can led to depression for many student-athletes. An increasing number of universities report that many of their student-athletes suffer from depression and anxiety disorders as they juggle practices, competitions, and academic demands. For some athletes, like former Division I swimmer Tiffany Clay, the stress of it all can blindside them.

ety and

ome an

Recruited to swim for the University of Tennessee, Clay found her life spinning out of control a month into her freshman year when she began suffering from migraines and had difficulty sleeping. Her course work became challenging and she lacked her usual drive and motivation in swim practice. Luckily for Clay, the university had a system in place to help students adjust to the stress and pressures of being an elite college athlete. When Clay's performance dropped, her coach suggested she contact a social worker at the university. Social workers at the university are part of a larger team of doctors, athletic trainers, sports psychologists, and academic counselors. Clay went on to become an All-American swimmer for the university and, eventually, the first-ever female swimming head coach at Long Island University, Brooklyn.

Providing support to student-athletes is important. This is especially true for female athletes, who experience depression and anxiety at roughly twice the rate of men. Athletes are often perceived as being mentally tough and capable of solving problems. But when an athlete is spending nearly forty hours a week in practice or competition and still needs to stay on top of course work, the stress can be overwhelming. In extreme cases, some athletes have committed suicide. In one highly publicized case, Sarah Devens, a three-sport star athlete at Dartmouth College, killed herself the summer before her senior year of college in 1995.

That year, Devens would have been a team captain in field hockey, ice hockey, and lacrosse.

STUDENT-ATHLETES AND DRUG ABUSE

College student-athletes are considered to be at a greater risk for the abuse of alcohol and other drugs, such as steroids, diet aids, ephedrine, marijuana, and psychedelic drugs, than their non-athletic peers. Social pressures and added stress from maintaining grueling academic and athletic schedules are seen as the top reasons why some student-athletes engage in drug or alcohol abuse.

Female student-athletes are not exempt from this behavior. A recent study revealed the following facts about drug and alcohol abuse by college student-athletes:

- College athletes have higher rates of alcohol abuse than their non-athletic peers, with 33 percent of female student-athletes reporting participation in binge drinking.
- Of the female student-athletes who reported being victims of sexual aggression, 68 percent reported that their assailants had been drinking at the time of the attack.
- Sixty-two percent of female collegiate gymnasts had used at least one extreme weight loss method

(diet pills, etc.) at least twice a week for three or more months.

- Approximately 30 percent of female student-athletes have admitted to using performance-enhancing drugs.

THE BENEFITS OF BEING A STUDENT-ATHLETE

While there are many challenges to being a student-athlete, including increased risk of alcohol abuse, stress, and anxiety, it's not all bad. It takes hard work and determination to succeed in sports, but there are many benefits to becoming involved in sports at any level. Women and girls who participate in sports report higher overall levels of confidence than their counterparts who do not. In general, women and girls who are active in sports (although not necessarily professionally or on the college-level) report higher levels of well-being and lower

There are many benefits to being a female athlete, including the strong relationships one can form with teammates and better health and well-being.

rates of depression. Other reported benefits include lower rates of obesity, a lower risk of cancer, higher reported grades and, later in life, better employment opportunities. Perhaps one of the most important benefits of women in sports is not rooted in individual experience at all. Women in sports today will inspire new generations of women who feel they can comfortably and successfully participate in the sport of their choice. The female athletes of today will become role models for the strong, dedicated, and athletic young women of tomorrow.

AESTHETIC Relating to or dealing with the beautiful; pleasing in appearance; attractive; appreciative or responsive to the beautiful.

CISGENDER Used to describe a person who identifies with the sex they were assigned at birth.

DISCRIMINATION Prejudiced or prejudicial outlook, action, or treatment.

EMPOWERMENT To give official authority or legal power for recommending a particular product.

ENDURANCE The ability to sustain a prolonged stressful effort or activity.

EQUALITY A state in which all people have the same status, level of respect, and rights.

GENDER A range of social and cultural characteristics used to distinguish between males and females.

HETEROSEXISM Discrimination or prejudice by heterosexuals against homosexuals.

INFERIOR Lower in station, rank, degree, or grade.

INTERCOLLEGIATE Existing, carried on, or participating in activities between colleges.

LEGISLATION A law that has been enacted by a government body.

PERFORMANCE-ENHANCING DRUGS (PEDS) Commonly known as PEDs, any number of substances that are used by athletes to improve performance ability, which can include drugs ranging from vitamins to steroids.

SOCIOLOGY The science of society, social institutions, and social relationships; the systematic study of the development, structure, interaction, and collective behavior of organized groups of human beings.

SPECTATOR A non-participatory observer of a sports event.

SPECULATION The act of meditating on or pondering a subject; the reviewing of something idly and often inconclusively.

STEREOTYPE Something conforming to a fixed or general pattern; a standardized mental picture that is held in common by members of a group and that represents an oversimplified opinion, prejudiced attitude, or uncritical judgment.

STEROID Any of various chemical compounds that include numerous hormones; any of several human-made hormones that are used in medicine to help tissue grow and that are sometimes abused by athletes to increase muscle size and strength and that may have harmful effects, such as stunted growth in teens.

SUBJECTIVE Characteristic of or belonging to reality as it is perceived by the human mind; relating to experience or knowledge as conditioned by personal mental states or characteristics; peculiar to a particular individual; personal; modified or affected by personal views, experience, or background.

TRANSGENDER Used to describe someone who does not identify or identify exclusively with the sex they were assigned at birth.

Canadian Association for the Advancement
of Women and Sport and Physical Activity
(CAAWS)
11 Marjory Avenue
Toronto, ON, M4M 2Y2
Canada
(416) 901-0484
Email: caaws@caaws.ca
Website: www.caaws.ca
Facebook: @CAAWS
Twitter: @CAAWS
CAAWS provides leadership and education
and builds capacity to foster equitable
support, diverse opportunities, and positive
experiences for girls and women in sports and
physical activity.

Images of Us (IOU) Sports
1531 W. Vliet Street
Milwaukee, WI 53205
(414) 934-0773
Email: info@iousports.org
Website: www.iousports.org
Facebook: @IOUSports
Twitter: @IOUSports
IOU Sports provides sports education, fitness
opportunities, career information, and
charitable assistance to girls and women

who participate in all levels of sports. The organization's goal is to empower girls using sports as an avenue that instills discipline, teamwork, and physical fitness to create well-rounded individuals.

National Council of Youth Sports (NCYS)
7185 Southeast Seagate Lane
Stuart, FL 34997
(772) 781-1452
Website: www.ncys.org
Facebook: @ncys.org
Twitter: @youthsportsNCYS
NCYS advocates the promotion of healthy lifestyles and safe environments for stronger neighborhoods and communities while enhancing the youth sports experience in America.

U Sports
45 Vogell Road, Suite 701
Richmond Hill, ON L4B 3P6
Canada
(905) 508-3000
Website: en.usports.ca
Facebook: @USportsCanada
Twitter: @USPORTSca
U Sports is the national association of university

sports in Canada. Member universities of
U Sports commit themselves to excellence
in their sports programs, optimize their
schedules, and assign coaches to year-round
programs to assist the federal government
in identifying talent. They also offer national
training centers, provisions for facilities,
sport research, and testing, all with an eye on
developing international competitors.

WomenSport International (WSI)
PO Box 743
Vashon, WA
Website: www.sportsbiz.bz
/womensportinternational/index.htm
WSI was formed to ensure that sports and
physical activity receive the attention and
priority they deserve in the lives of girls and
women and to bring about positive change for
girls and women in these important areas of
their lives.

Women's Sports Foundation
247 West 30th Street, Suite 7R
New York, NY 10001
(646) 845-0273
Website: www.womenssportsfoundation.org

Facebook: @WomensSportsFoundation
Twitter: @WomensSportsFdn
Founded in 1974 by tennis legend Billie Jean
King, the Women's Sports Foundation is
dedicated to advancing the lives of girls and
women through sports and physical activity.

WEBSITES

Due to the changing nature of internet links,
Rosen Publishing has developed an online list of
websites related to the subject of this book. This
site is updated regularly. Please use this link to
access this list:

http://www.rosenlinks.com/WITW/Athlete

Allen, Kathy and Yolanda L. Jackson. *Girls Race!: Amazing Tales of Women in Sports* (Girls Rock!). North Mankato, MN: Capstone Press, 2013.

Bildner, Phil and Brett Helquist. *Martina & Chrissie: The Greatest Rivalry in the History of Sports.* Somerville, MA: Candlewick, 2017.

Christopher, Matt. *Great Americans in Sports: Mia Hamm.* New York, NY: Little, Brown Books for Young Readers, 2015.

Dunn, Mary R. *Michelle Wie* (Women in Sports). North Mankato, MN: Capstone Press, 2016.

Ignotofsky, Rachel. *Women in Sports: 50 Fearless Athletes Who Played to Win.* Berkeley, CA: Ten Speed Press, 2017.

Lewis, Angela. *Post Moves: The Female Athlete's Guide to Dominate Life After College.* Global Athlete Media Network, 2016.

Millbern Powers, Debbie. *Meeting Her Match: The Story of a Female Athlete-Coach, Before and After Title IX.* CreateSpace, 2014.

Porter, Esther. *Serena Williams* (Women in Sports). North Mankato, MN: Capstone Press, 2016.

Savage, Jeff. *Danica Patrick* (Amazing Athletes). New York, NY: Scholastic, 2013.

Schiot, Molly. *Game Changers: The Unsung Heroines of Sports History.* New York, NY: Simon & Schuster, 2016.

Brown, Ryan. "What's on TV: Not Women's
    Sports." *Salon*, July 13, 2010. http://www.salon.
    com/2010/07/13/womens_sports_not_on_tv.
"Danica Drives Racing Ratings and Buzz." *Nielson
    Newswire*, February 24, 2012. http://www.
    nielsen.com/us/en/insights/news/2012
    /danica-drives-racing-ratings-and-buzz.html.
Das, Andrew. "Pay Disparity in U.S. Soccer? It's
    Complicated." *New York Times,* April 21, 2016.
    https://www.nytimes.com/2016/04/22/sports
    /soccer/usmnt-uswnt-soccer-equal-pay.html.
Dusenbery, Maya and Jaeah Lee. "Charts: The
    State of Women's Athletics, 40 Years After Title
    IX." *Mother Jones*, June 22, 2012. http://www
    .motherjones.com/politics/2012/06/charts
    -womens-athletics-title-nine-ncaa.
Ellis, Jena. "Biggest Milestones in U.S. Women's
    Sports History." *SportsThenAndNow.com*,
    July 23, 2011. http://sportsthenandnow
    .com/2011/07/23/biggest-milestones-in
    -u-s-womens-sports-history.
ESPN Staff. "New Mexico Player Banned,
    Apologizes." *ESPN*, November 6, 2009.
    http://sports.espn.go.com/ncaa/news
    /story?id=4629837.
Ferguson, Doug. "Wie Has Better Balance in Her
    Life." *St. Louis Post-Dispatch*, February 15,
    2012. http://www.stltoday.com/sports/golf
    /wie-has-better-balance-in-her-life

/article_8e21e00a-dbcc-5241-8f42
-00f05fec0717.html.

Ferreras, Jesse. "'Cover The Athlete' Urges Media
To Stop Asking Women Sexist Questions."
Huffington Post Canada, November 6, 2015.
http://www.huffingtonpost.ca/2015/11/06
/cover-the-athlete-sexist-
questions_n_8483906.html.

Gardiner, Andy. "Suffering from Depression."
USA Today, February 5, 2006. http://www
.usatoday.com/news/health/2006-02-05
-womens-health-depression_x.htm.

Gavin, Mary L. "5 Reasons for Girls to Play
Sports." *KidsHealth.org*. May 2011. http://
kidshealth.org/teen/food_fitness/sports/girls
_sports.html.

Gottesman, Jane. *Game Face: What Does a Female
Athlete Look Like?* New York, NY: Random
House Trade Paperbacks, 2003.

Hellmich, Nanci. "Athletes' Hunger to Win Fuels
Eating Disorders." *USA Today*, February 5, 2006.
http://www.usatoday.com/news/health/2006
-02-05-women-health-cover_x.htm.

Kane, Mary Jo. "Sex Sells Sex, Not Women's Sports."
Pittsburgh Post-Gazette, August 28, 2011. http://
www.post-gazette.com/pg/11240/1170120
-109-0.stm?cmpid=newspanel6.

Koehler, Michael. *Advising Student Athletes Through the College Recruitment Process.* New York, NY: Prentice Hall, 1996.

McDonagh, Eileen, and Laura Pappano. *Playing with the Boys: Why Separate Is Not Equal in Sports.* New York, NY: Oxford University Press, 2009.

Pappano, Laura, and Eileen McDonagh. "Women and Men in Sports: Separate But Not Equal." *Christian Science Monitor,* January 31, 2008. http://www.csmonitor.com/Commentary /Opinion/2008/0131/p09s01-coop.html

Plummer, William. "Dying For a Medal." *People Magazine,* August 22, 1994. http://www. people.com/people/archive /article/0,,20103704,00.html.

Rotondi, Jessica Pearce. "Danica Patrick and the 'Danica Effect.'" *Huffington Post,* February 27, 2012. http://www.huffingtonpost.com /jessica-pearce-rotondi/danica-patrick -danica-effect_b_1305443.html.

Schwartz, Larry. "Martina Was Alone On Top." *ESPN.* Retrieved March 9, 2017. http://espn.go.com/sportscentury /features/00016378.html.

Shipley, Amy. "Jones Pleads Guilty, Admits Using Steroids." *Washington Post,* October 6, 2007. http://www.washingtonpost.com/wp-dyn

/content/story/2007/10/05/ST2007100502097
.html?sid=ST2007100502097.

Stenson, Jacqueline. "Kids on Steroids Willing
to Risk It All For Success." *MSNBC*, March 3,
2008. http://www.msnbc.msn.com
/id/22984780/ns/health-childrens_health
/t/kids-steroids-willing-risk-it-all-success
/#.T05G8szs2xE.

Suarez Sang, Lucia I. "Only Latina on U.S.
Women's World Cup Team, Amy Rodriguez,
Hopes to Inspire Others." *Fox News*, June 8,
2015. http://www.foxnews.com
/sports/2015/06/08/surrounded-by
-great-talent-amy-rodriguez-looks-to
-shine-at-womens-world-cup.html.

Sylwester, MaryJo. "Culture, Family Play Role in
Sports for Latina Girls." *USA Today*, March 29,
2005. http://www.usatoday.com/sports/2005
-03-28-hispanic-tradition_x.htm.

Tapia, Andres. "U.S. Women's Soccer: Not Quite
America's Team." *New America Media*, July 27,
2011. http://newamericamedia.org/2011/07
/us-womens-soccer-not-quite-americas
-team.php.

"Title IX, Back on Track." *New York Times*,
April 20, 2010. http://www.nytimes
.com/2010/04/21/opinion/21wed3.html.

Williams, Lena. "Hispanic Female Athletes
Few and Far Between." *Puerto Rico Herald*,
November 6, 2002. http://www
.puertorico-herald.org/issues/2002/vol6n46
/HispFemaleAthlet-en.html.

Women's Sports Foundation. "Mythbusting:
What Every Female Athlete Should Know."
Retrieved March 9, 2017. http://www
.womenssportsfoundation.org/en/sitecore
/content/home/athletes/for-athletes/know
-your-rights/athlete-resources/mythbusting
-what-every-female-athlete-should
-know.aspx.

Woods, Jewel. "Venus and Serena Williams:
Ousted By Racism." *Huffington Post*,
February 27, 2009. http://www.huffingtonpost
.com/jewel-woods/venus-and-serena
-williams_b_169927.html.

INDEX

ABOUT THE AUTHORS

Lena Koya is a writer who also enjoys running, hiking, practicing yoga, and generally staying active. She also enjoys kicking around a soccer ball with her young son. She lives with her family in the New York Metro area.

Laura La Bella is a lifelong runner who recently took up cycling and is mastering the art of kayaking. She is a writer who lives, works, paddles, and runs in and around Rochester, New York.

PHOTO CREDITS

Cover Artiga Photo/Corbis/Getty Images; pp. 6–7 Kevin C. Cox/Getty Images; p. 11 Pacific Press/Light Rocket/Getty Images; p. 13 Hulton Deutsch Collection/Corbis Historical/ Getty Images; p. 15 Bettmann/Getty Images; p. 20 Ronald Martinez/Getty Images; p. 23 Todd Pennington/Getty Images; p. 25 Don Emmert/AFP/Getty Images; pp. 28–29, 32–33 Harry How/Getty Images; pp. 38–39 Linda Spillers/Getty Images; pp. 42–43 Richard T. Gagnon/Getty Images; p. 45 The Boston Globe/Getty Images; p. 47 Icon Sports Wire/Getty Images; pp. 52–53 Echo/Juice Images/Getty Images; p. 55 Michael Loccisano/FilmMagic/Getty Images; p. 59 Kirby Lee/ Getty Images; p. 62 Jim Rogash/Getty Images; p. 66 Alain Grosclaude/Agence Zoom/Getty Images; p. 68 Jason Squires/ Getty Images; p. 72 Brian To/FilmMagic/Getty Images; p. 76 Jerod Harris/WireImage/Getty Images; pp. 78–79 Clive Brunskill/Getty Images; p. 83 Gregory Shamus/Getty Images; p. 87 Mel Melcon/Los Angeles Times/Getty Images; p. 89 NCAA Photos/Getty Images; pp. 92–93 Laurence Griffiths/ Getty Images; cover and interior pages (globe) LuckyDesigner/ Shutterstock.com; cover and interior pages background designs lulias/Shutterstock.com, Dawid Lech/Shutterstock.com, Transia Design/Shutterstock.com.

Design & Layout: Nicole Russo-Duca; Editor & Photo Research: Elizabeth Schmermund